FROM BROKE TO BANK: STEP BY STEP GUIDE TO HOME BASED AEROBIC CENTER CONSULTING BUSINESS

Soham M.

Copyright © 2018

All rights reserved. No part of this book may be reproduced or transmitted in any form or by any means, electronic or mechanical, including photocopying, recording or by any information storage and retrieval system without written permission of the publisher, except for the inclusion of brief quotations in a review.

Disclaimer:

Please read the Disclaimer carefully before you read this book. You accept and agree to be bound and abide by the Disclaimer. The information contained on this book is for educational and informational purposes only. The information contained on this book is not intended as, and shall not be understood or construed as, professional advice.

The brand names or logos discussed in this book are property of their respective owners.

Introduction..5
How to approach the client 6
Why you must be hired as a marketing consultant .9
Market research..12
Preparing promotional strategies for your client ..14
Working with an independent contractor, what you must know..19
Preparing reports for the client 21
The power of seminars..24
The power of testimonials.......................................26

Introduction

This book discusses the business of providing marketing consultancy to the aerobics center. An aerobics center offers the physical exercises that are designed to improve the fitness in terms of muscle strength and cardiovascular fitness in the individual. An aerobic center business is highly localized and requires a marketing strategy that is different from product or service that can has the potential to reach to the higher demographic area.

An aerobic center requires innovative marketing solutions that can market the fitness products to various groups. Usually, the owners of the aerobics centers take care of the marketing process themselves. Your job as a marketing consultant is to convince them to hire you as an external marketing consultant, by highlighting the potential benefits their business can receive. Usually, the owners of the small and localized business have several misconceptions about appointing a marketing consultant and diving into the digital marketing sphere to expand their business.

How to approach the client

When you approach the client for the first time, you must have a very pleasing attitude. Do not approach the client on the first meeting with the sole intention of selling, you will be disappointed. Instead, make the meeting an enjoyable experience for you as well as the client. Before approaching the client you must do the market research and must have an answer as to why the aerobics center requires your services. It would be wise to spend some time analyzing his website if he has any, if he has a website then you are in luck because there are several free website analysis tools available on the internet. You can list out various sections that require an improvement and also suggest ways to improve the same. You must perform a through analysis of the Facebook page of your client, weather the page design is aesthetic and appealing if the page is updated on regular basis with interesting content, pictures or videos, what kind of interaction is happening between your client and Facebook users. This type of research will give you enough ammunition to keep your client interested in the conversation because you are going to talk about his business, and anything related to his business is bound to interest him. You can send this free report to your client and demonstrate your commitment towards your work. Your prospective client will definitely be impressed if you put in some effort to understand his business and offer a solution to improve it.

It is important to prepare a good opening statement when you meet your client. Some people fumble in their openers, some stress too much importance on introducing themselves while some stress on greeting the client. Ideally, you must great your client along with something to talk about his business or how your product or service is going to benefit his business; you must be quick to make a transition to question or dialogue that initiates the conversation and make the client comfortable as soon as possible.

Many people advocate that preparing the sales script is no longer considered fashionable. This is wrong because a sales script enables you to prepare an effective communication strategy by highlighting all the probable questions that your client might ask or it is even possible that without a sales script you might leave out something that is very important for the business of a client.

If you are inexperienced or have approach anxiety then it is advisable to practice the sales script several times until you become confident because if you know your script very well then it will naturally boost your confidence and it will not look like you're trying hard to impress the client.

The sales script also helps you to prepare in advance answer any questions that a client might ask regarding his business. If you are well prepared then your client will be comfortable talking to you or even working with you if you demonstrate enough confidence and knowledge about his business.

Remember that you are not going to make a sale on the first contact, try to act natural and pleasant as if you didn't approach the client with the sole intention of getting the business from him. You will require doing regular follow-ups with the client. It is very important that your body language or tone of the voice don't appear aggressive.

Try to build a good relationship with the client, demonstrate your willingness to help him if the need arises.

Why you must be hired as a marketing consultant

Many business owners think that they do not require a marketing consultant; it is your job to prove them wrong. In your first meeting you have already provided a free report highlighting the areas that require improvements, now it is time to stress on how you can help your client to leverage his experience for the growth of his business. Usually, people are comfortable working with those who have a proven track record and backed by educational qualifications.

You must highlight the projects that you have completed successfully in the past. If you have a satisfied list of clients then you will not have to try hard, but if you don't have any experience then you will have to convince your client to trust you, and this could be tricky.

You can point out to your client that you have a team of specialists, and if he wishes, he can have the opportunity to work with a specialized consultancy firm with a good reputation, but the expense of working with such firm would be quite high. It would be profitable for a local business to hire a freelance marketing consultant because of the flexibility it offers like hiring for a specific purpose, for example, your client can hire you for a specific marketing activity like digital marketing.

Since you have already provided your prospective client with a free report highlighting the areas that require improvement, you can stress on the fact that appointing an external marketing consultant can bring the outside perspective that could benefit his business immensely. The small business owner who is taking care of the marketing activity himself or having an in-house marketing team will always have a biased approach towards any marketing activity. You can point out that you, as an external marketer can bring clarity in his vision of the business.

You can also point out that you have access to the best talent in web developing, graphic designing, or copywriting. If a specialized set of skills are available then it will do wonders for your client's marketing campaigns. You could also stress the fact that if your client chooses then he can appoint you for a very short term assignment that could include offering suggestions for improvement in various areas of his business or handling the particular marketing campaign to attract new customers.
This will be cheaper than hiring an employee for a full-time basis.

If your client hires you then he will have more time available to focus on his core business and this will eventually lead to increased customer satisfaction. Even on the operational front, the decision to appoint you will lead to more focus on the operations of the company, this will enable him to identify the problems in his business in its initial stages and devise a solution to prevent it becoming a big headache later on.

Hiring an external marketing consultant will also lead to the increased accountability. As a business owner if he decides to do the things his way then there are chances that he might lose track and make wrong decisions because he is not accountable to anyone for his actions. An external marketing consultant will set up the goals and follow them diligently and if these goals are not achieved then the owner of the aerobics center can always demand an explanation.

Market research

Once you are hired as a marketing consultant, your goal is to maximize the return on investment for your client. You must perform market research because it will give you a clear picture on the areas that you must focus on for your client. For example, you can start visiting other aerobics center in the area and find out the schemes offered by them to their existing as well and new customers. You also have to research the various aerobic programs offered by them to their clients and compare them with your client's offers. You must also visit the website of the competitors and sign up for any offers or promotions so that you can keep track of what your client needs to do to beat the competition.

You must also try to find out how the competitors are serving various target groups like students, housewife or elderly people. Your goal must be to bridge the gap between your client's aerobics center and his competitor's aerobics center. You must analyze the process of delivering the service to the customers. You can prepare a comprehensive chart highlighting various components of successful aerobics center and try to emulate the same with your client's aerobics center. For example, you can visit various aerobics center and observe the ambience of their clinics, their staff's competence in handling customer queries or complaints, how far the competitors go to make their clients happy and so on. List all these factors and compare them with your client's aerobics center. This will give you an idea of the changes to be made to the operational structure of the client.

Next, you must observe the marketing campaigns undertaken by the competitors. For example, you can study the design and presentation of the competitor's brochure and flyers, what kind of message are they stressing to the prospective customer, what kind of services are prominently advertised by them and so on. You can prepare a comparison chart by listing every aspect of the competitor's efforts to attract new customers and your clients aerobics center and you must incorporate all the good elements of the competitors into your clients aerobics center.

You must also research for any positive or negative reviews that your client's business might have received from its customers on the internet. If the reviews are present then you will have to analyze them and prepare a report if there is any need to take action.

Preparing promotional strategies for your client

Today's consumers are more aware about their fitness, they also want to join the aerobics center that is not only modern but also provides excellent customer service.

People love to take up the trial offers especially offered by fitness center like aerobics. If the aerobics center offers free trial then not only people can visit the center and enjoy the facilities without having to pay any money upfront, but they can also get a opportunity to experience a quality of the environment in the aerobics center. This is an opportunity for the aerobics center to showcase the excellence in their services. If people are satisfied in the trial session then they will surely join the aerobics center.

The best salespeople are customers themselves, the aerobics center can encourage the customers to bring along their friends for a free trial. In return, the aerobics center can provide some form of incentive to the customer for referring his friend. These kinds of incentive go along way in increasing the customer loyalty. If the referral joins the aerobic center then the original referrer can be rewarded with free membership for a month.

In the digital age, it is very important that the aerobics center does not neglect the importance of online presence. Many customers would prefer to book their appointments online. Hence the aerobic center can tie up with the online website to offer some sort of coupons to the initial customers who might want to try a session. Customers should also be encouraged to ask questions regarding the packages or the benefits of joining the aerobics center. This kind of interaction makes the customer comfortable. The aerobics center can organize the webinars for prospective customers so that if they have any doubts or queries it can be solved in the webinars. An aerobics center can even offer various diet plans for its customers as a complimentary service. This shows that the center cares for the fitness of the customer. This could be a top attraction because people would prefer the idea of eating tasty food and staying healthy.

An aerobics center can even use flyers for promoting their various offers or discounts scheme. Flyers can be used to create awareness about the benefits that the aerobic center provides to the customer including the competitive pricing and the facilities provided to the customer. The aerobics Center can even ask the customers to bring the flyers for availing the free session. This will ensure that people do not throw away the flyers and can even increase the response rate of the people.

The aerobic Center can even use postcards to reach its potential customers, even though some people think that the postcards are dead but this is far from the truth because even today people spend considerable time sifting through their physical mail then spending the same amount of time for electronic mail or email. Postcards gave the personal tint to the communication. A postcard is an ideal way to generate brand awareness or offer a rebate to the existing or prospective customers. It is very important to remember that the interaction through postcard should be fun; the message should be such that it captures the attention of the customer. Another advantage of the postcard is that it helps the customer to remember the name of the aerobics center, whenever the customer searches on the internet and if the name of the aerobic Center crops up then he will immediately recollect the postcard send by your client. Postcards are also an ideal way to reach new people who have recently shifted to the locality.

Social media websites offer an ideal platform to reach prospective customers and engage them in the meaningful conversations. The interaction on social media does not cost a dime. In fact, by networking with the people, the aerobics center can reach thousands of potential customers and engage them in one way or other. The aerobics Center can even start a fitness challenge where it can encourage the users to post their pictures or videos along with their daily goals. The winner of the fitness challenge could be offered a free membership for a month and the rest of the people who have participated in the challenge can be offered discount coupons to join various programs.

Social media website offers an opportunity for regular interaction, it is very important to reply to the message received from a prospective client, this way the conversation can build trust in the mind of the prospective customer which could convert later. The key is to maintain consistency and to be active on the social media.

Social media platform like Instagram can help to capture a large audience in the shortest possible time; all the aerobic Center has to do is to follow the influencers in their area or city. The aerobic center can even invite the influencers to visit the facility for free sessions and experience the ambience in the center. This should not be some sort of promotional campaign where the influencers are pressurized to post a picture or two about the aerobics center. Even leading bloggers or journalists from a local newspaper or magazine should be invited for free sessions at the aerobic center. They should be offered free diet plans as well, this could encourage them to write a few words about the aerobic center or post some pictures in their respective newspapers. This kind of campaigns can generate the buzz very quickly. The aerobic center can even tap into the minds of past customers. It is a known fact that when someone recollects the past memory, the effect usually is a pleasant one, and people would be willing to refer their friends or family members to the aerobics Center because of the pleasant memories they have.

If you have been a visitor of the shopping website then you must have noticed the popping messages that offer you an irresistible deal, some products that are worth $1100 are offered for just $699 if the customer purchases it at that particular moment or there is an offer that provides free installation of a certain product along with an extended warranty if the customer decides to buy the product immediately. These types of offers force the customers to take action or make them feel left out. By creating such offers the price becomes less important. What does an offer do? The offer provides solution to the particular problem, for example, if the customer buys the membership of the aerobic center then he will also get free diet plan or a free body mass index check up that would tell him if he is overweight or not and if he is overweight then the fitness center can provide him with solutions to make him fit and healthy.

The existing customers can also be encouraged to post a picture or a video of them having a great time at the aerobic center. In return, the aerobic Center can offer a certain rebate or free sessions in the center. Even if a few customers post such pictures in their social media accounts, it can go long way in reaching new potential customers.

Working with an independent contractor, what you must know

You will be working with a web developer, copywriter, graphic designer, etc. You could be working with one company or working with separate individuals, either way, you will have to follow the procedures properly while working with an independent contractor.
You will be required to establish the fact that the people you have worked with are independent contractors. Any misclassification on your part could lead to significant penalties later on.

Whenever you work with an independent contractor, you must ask for details such as weather they are working as a freelancer or have incorporated their company. Some might be operating on a sole proprietorship basis too. It is very important that you prepare proper documentation for hiring a freelancer or independent contractor. You must sign proper agreements to this effect, and the agreement must clearly mention the terms and conditions and the relationship you will be having with an independent contractor.

It is your responsibility to ask for the documentary proof such as his website or a business license or a business card that establishes him as an independent contractor. These precautions are required to protect you from any future audit from a government department. You must get form W-9 signed by every independent contractor before they begin their work. It is your responsibility to ask for proper tax ID, if they don't have a proper tax ID then you can withhold the tax payments. You will also be required to maintain the record of each payment given to an independent contractor because if the payment amount exceeds $600 in a year then such payment information has to be notified by filling the form 1099-MISC. always keep in mind that it is your responsibility to protect yourself from any legal hassles later on.

Preparing reports for the client

As a marketing consultant you have to be aware of what is working and what is not, as your client, the aerobic center would also be interested in knowing the same. You will be required to prepare a comprehensive report detailing each task that has been undertaken by you and the end result of such a task. In a large organization, every department has to furnish periodic reports about the working of their departments. Such reports are compiled in too much larger reports that enable the organization to take effective decisions. Reports are also necessary because they provide an insight into various campaigns and the return on investment generated by each campaign. A Report enables the client to see the results of the money spent by him on hiring professionals for his business. Reports also highlight those areas where results are visible for example in SEO the result could be visible only after a certain period of time that's why they cannot be quantified on paper immediately, on the other hand, the results of PPC campaign are visible immediately and its effect can be seen on the website in terms of visitor engagement.

The report could focus on the following:

Increase in traffic volumes of the website

Increase in transactional volumes in terms of queries or free sign up

The conversion rate for the money spent on various campaigns

The source of the traffic, this tells the owner about the origin of queries whether they are from a website or mobile device.

Reach of the content that explains which type of content the visitor was interested most.

A number of social shares that can enable the client to view the effect pictures or videos generated from ordinary people.

Provide insights on the onsite engagement of the customer, this explains what was the bounce rate or the average time spent by the customer on the website and the sections which interested him most.

Search visibility of the website, this shows how the website ranks for the particular keyword and how it performs compared to some competitors in search engines.

While preparing report it is very important to have a correct data on hand because if the data is distorted then the report too will be far off the mark in providing a correct picture to the client.

You can even use the graph to represent various data sets because graphical representation can make it easier for the client to read and understand the report. You can even highlight the graph where the major changes are visible; this helps you to capture major fluctuations that have occurred because of some event or effort. You can even add your own commentary to each section explaining the reasons for success or failure in that particular segment at a particular time. A commentary with an interesting headline can make a report very interesting to read.

It is up to you as a consultant to decide whether to provide the reports on a weekly or monthly basis. You will have to prepare a final report at the end of the campaign and this report should be discussed face to face with your client.

The power of seminars

Seminars are the best way to reach and interact with the potential customers. You can advise the client to organize a free seminar in the neighborhood on Sunday to educate people about the importance of fitness and remaining healthy. In the seminar, the aerobic center can explain in depth about the services offered by them for various groups and the benefits of each service. For example, a package for weight loss can be explained to the housewives and how can they utilize their afternoon time to stay fit with just 45 minutes of fun-filled exercises. If it is possible the aerobic center can even arrange a small demonstration of the exercises to be performed by the staff, inviting even a few people from the audience on the stage to perform some exercises. This will make the people feel as if they are part of the exercises and can experience the thrill or fun of doing them.

A question-answer session can be organized so that if people have any queries or doubts then they can be answered by the aerobic center specialists. This kind of interaction builds trust and confidence in the mind of the customer. People are more likely to join the aerobic center if they feel that they would be taken care of by a fitness expert. A well trained and courteous staff can help to build a positive impression in the mind of the customer.

If it is possible, the past customers can also be invited to share their experiences they had with the aerobics center. A customer having pleasant memories can provide a huge image boost for the aerobics center.

The key is to make people comfortable and assure them that they are in the best hands.

The power of testimonials

Testimonials are a great way to demonstrate the dedication and commitment of the aerobic center towards its customers. A happy customer is the sign that he is taken care of very well by the aerobics center. If the customer speaks highly for the aerobic center then it conveys the message that the aerobics center not only cares for its customers but also provides an experience that is fun-filled and enjoyable.

People are always suspicious of the claims made by the companies in their advertisements but when it comes to customer feedback they will even trust a stranger. The testimonial reaffirms the customer's decision to buy the membership. He knows that he has done the right thing and this puts him on the ease.

It would be a great thing if the aerobic center can convince its customers to provide video testimonials. Video testimonials have an everlasting impact and can make the customer feel the emotions of the speaker. Thus if the speaker is feeling happy and satisfied then the prospective customer who is viewing the video will also feel happier, and there is a better chance of the potential customer ending up becoming the member of the aerobics center. Videos also have high retention power so if the prospective customer has viewed the video then there is a chance that he might remember the name of the aerobic centre for a long time even if he doesn't become the member immediately.

More Books In The Series

STEP BY STEP GUIDE TO SURVIVE AS COPYWRITER

STEP BY STEP GUIDE TO PET SITTING BUSINESS

STEP BY STEP GUIDE TO DIGITAL MARKETING CONSULTING BUSINESS

STEP BY STEP GUIDE TO DENTAL CLINIC MARKETING CONSULTING BUSINESS

STEP BY STEP GUIDE TO RESAURANT MARKETING CONSULTING BUSINESS

STEP BY STEP GUIDE TO YOGA CENTER CONSULTING BUSINESS

www.ingramcontent.com/pod-product-compliance
Lightning Source LLC
Chambersburg PA
CBHW032311240526
45464CB00023BA/2984